BLUEBERRIES

ELAINE ELLIOT AND VIRGINIA LEE

Photographed on location by Steven Isleifson

FORMAC PUBLISHING COMPANY LIMITED

PHOTO CREDITS:
All photographs by Steven Isleifson except where noted below:
Keith Vaughan — pages 1, 3 (top,) 4, 5, 58, 59

PARTICIPATING RESTAURANTS:

Acton's Grill and Café, Wolfville, NS

Amherst Shore Country Inn, Lorneville, NS

Bellhill Tea House, Canning, NS

Blomidon Inn, Wolfville, NS

Bluenose Lodge, Lunenburg, NS

Bright House, Sherbrooke, NS

Compass Rose Inn, Lunenburg, NS

Dalvay-by-the-Sea, Dalvay, PEI

Drury Lane Steak House, Aulac, NB

Dufferin Inn and San Martello Diningroom, Saint John, NB

Duncreigan Country Inn, Mabou, NS

Dunes Café and Gardens, Brackley Beach, PEI

Falcourt Inn, Nictaux, NS

Garrison House Inn, Annapolis Royal, NS

Gowrie House Country Inn, Sydney Mines, NS

Haddon Hall, Chester, NS

Inn at Bay Fortune, Bay Fortune, PEI

Inn on the Cove, Saint John, NB

Inn on the Lake, Waverley, NS

Keltic Lodge, Ingonish, NS

La Perla Restaurant, Dartmouth, NS

Marshlands Inn, Sackville, NB

Mountain Gap Inn, Smith's Cove, NS

Pines Resort Hotel, Digby, NS

Quaco Inn, St. Martins, NB

Sweet Lou's Dessert Café, Halifax, NS

Dedication:

This book is dedicated to the memory of our parents, Margaret and Frank Stuart, who instilled in us a love of the Maritime way of life and taught us to believe in ourselves.

Formac Publishing Company Limited acknowledges the support of the Department of Canadian Heritage and the Nova Scotia Department of Education and Culture in the development of writing and publishing in Canada.

Canadian Cataloguing in Publication Data

Elliot, Elaine, 1939-
      Blueberries
      (Maritime flavours series)
      ISBN 0-88780-350-4

1. Cookery (Blueberries). 2. Cookery, Canadian -- Maritime Provinces.
I. Lee, Virginia, 1947- . II. Title. III. Series.
TX813.B5E44 1996   641.6'4737   C95-950017-3

Formac Publishing Company Limited
5502 Atlantic Street
Halifax, N.S.
B3H 1G4

Distributed in the United States by:
Seven Hills Book Distributors
49 Central Avenue
Cincinnati, OH   45202

CONTENTS

INTRODUCTION

The very warm reception accorded our book, *Maritime Flavours Guidebook and Cookbook*, demonstrated that interest in the cuisine of the Maritime region is flourishing. The book also showed how you can prepare at home innovative recipes that professional chefs have developed in all three provinces.

In our visits to inns and restaurants over the years, one thing that has impressed us is the wide range of ideas that our best chefs have for including regional specialities. For this reason we decided to develop a series of four books that would celebrate the wonderful bounty of land and sea, in particular apples, blueberries, salmon, and lobster and other shellfish. We visited many of the inns and restaurants featured in *Maritime Flavours* and once again, the chefs gave us a generous selection of recipes with which to work. We selected the ones that would give you a wide range of choice for enjoying the flavours of the region. To round out each book, we added some tried and true recipes from our personal collections. All recipes in this book have been tested in our homes and the quantities adjusted to serve four to six adults. For some recipes we have suggested low-fat alternatives.

Fine food presentation is an art, and one which is receiving increased emphasis by our chefs. What better way to describe how these recipes are presented by their originators than to show you! Photographer Steven Isleifson visited our featured restaurants and photographed the dishes found in this *Maritime Flavours* series. What you see in these pages are the dishes as they are presented by their chefs, photographed on location.

Blueberries have been a specialty in the region for a very long time and we have a bountiful supply of ideas for serving these tasty berries. Sometimes these are classics, such as

Blueberry Grunt from the Mountain Gap Inn in Smith's Cove, NS, some are innovations, like Assorted Greens with Blueberry Vinaigrette from the Amherst Shore Country Inn in Lorneville, NS, or Roast Loin of Pork with Blueberry and Juniper Sauce from the Dunes Café and Gardens, Brackley Beach, PEI.

The blueberry, and its relatives, the huckleberry and cranberry, are indigenous to Atlantic Canada. Native North Americans and early European settlers extended the season for enjoying blueberries by sun-drying them for winter use.

Summer means berries and berry picking! We fondly remember, when growing up in rural Nova Scotia, those warm sunny days in August when we would go to the berry barrens as a family. Enticed by the prospect of warm blueberry pie, we would pick and pick, filling our pails and passing a whole afternoon in the open air.

Canada is the world's largest commercial producer of blueberries, with exports valued at over $40 million for the wild variety and $8 million for high-bush varieties. Atlantic Canada's climate and acidic soil are well suited for blueberry production.

Commercially grown and harvested berries are available at fruit stands and supermarkets from mid-August through September, and quick frozen berries are available year-round. The small commercial berries are grown in the wild under controlled agricultural management. These berries are harvested by hand or machine and provide seasonal jobs for hundreds of Canadians. The large, plump commercial blueberries are a high-bush hybrid developed from the wild variety during this

century. Cultivators were able to increase the size, quality and growing season of this berry without sacrificing its delicious wild flavour.

As in the past, we were pleasantly surprised by the versatility of our contributing chefs. Always eager to utilize local produce, they have shown great ingenuity incorporating this berry in their recipes. In this book you will find breakfast treats, appetizers, main course entrées and wonderful desserts.

SELECTION

Blueberries range in colour from light blue to blue-black and will often have a slight powdery cast over the blue. They should be picked only when fully ripe and plump. Handle berries with care as they easily bruise and for optimum quality store no more than 2-3 days in the refrigerator. Do not wash berries before use as they will deteriorate and spoil.

Frozen berries can be purchased year-round. Look for "I.Q.F." (individual quick frozen) mark on the container. This ensures a quality product. We have found you can interchange frozen berries for fresh in most recipes.

NUTRITIONAL VALUE

Known as the dieter's delight, blueberries are an excellent source of Vitamin A, are low in sodium and totally lack cholesterol. They also provide Vitamin C, calcium, phosphorous, potassium and are a source of dietary fibre. A one-cup serving of fresh blueberries contains only 81 calories yet supplies one-third of an adult's daily requirements of Vitamin C.

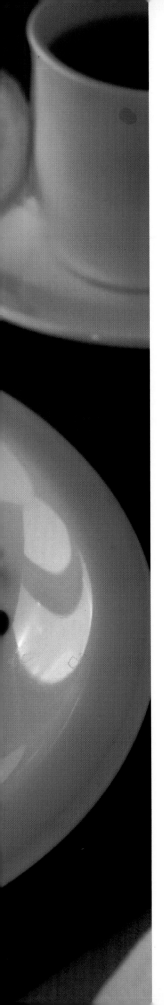

BREAKFAST

What better way to start a day than to sit down to a bowl of fresh blueberries. Or perhaps you would like to sample Sweet Lou's Lowfat Blueberry Muffins? But for that special weekend breakfast, be sure to try Blueberry Pancakes topped with Maritime maple syrup!

◄ *Blueberry Cinnamon Coffee Cake from the Inn on the Lake, Waverley, NS.*

BLUEBERRY CINNAMON COFFEE CAKE

INN ON THE LAKE, WAVERLEY, NS

*Blueberry season is a special time at the Inn on the Lake: chef Terry Provo adapts
a variety of different recipes to include the Maritime blueberry.*

1 cup fresh blueberries

1 teaspoon cinnamon

1/2 cup butter

1 cup sugar

2 eggs

1 1/2 teaspoons vanilla

1 1/2 cups flour

2 teaspoons baking powder

1/4 teaspoon salt

2/3 cup milk

Blueberry Sauce (recipe follows)

whipped cream as garnish (optional)

Preheat oven to 350°F. Toss blueberries with cinnamon and set aside. Cream butter and sugar together until fluffy. Beat in eggs, one at a time; add vanilla. Sift together flour, baking powder and salt. Add flour to butter mixture, alternately with milk, in three additions. Fold in blueberries. Pour batter into a greased 10-inch round spring form pan and bake for 40–45 minutes. Cake is ready when a toothpick inserted in the centre comes out clean. Let cool for 20 minutes, unmold and serve with warm Blueberry Sauce and whipped cream. Serves 10–12.

Blueberry Sauce

1 cup blueberries

1 cup sugar

1 tablespoon cornstarch, mixed in 1/4 cup cold water

Combine all ingredients in a saucepan, bring to a boil and cook until thickened. Serve warm over coffee cake.

LOWFAT BLUEBERRY MUFFINS

SWEET LOU'S DESSERT CAFÉ, HALIFAX, NS

Chef Pamela Veliath brought this recipe to Sweet Lou's from Cape Breton. They have become not only a healthy choice but an all-time favourite of her customers.

3 1/2 cups flour

1 tablespoon baking powder

1/2 teaspoon baking soda

1/2 teaspoon salt

2 eggs, beaten

1/2 cup vegetable oil

1/2 cup brown sugar

1 3/4 cup unsweetened applesauce

3/4 cup blueberries

1/2 cup cranberries, chopped (optional)

1/4 cup brown sugar, 2nd amount

Preheat oven to 375°F. Sift flour, baking powder, soda and salt into a large mixing bowl. In a separate bowl, whisk together eggs, oil, brown sugar and applesauce; add to dry ingredients and mix until just blended. Fold berries into the batter and pour into prepared muffin tins, filling two-thirds full. Sprinkle tops with brown sugar (2nd amount) and bake for 20–25 minutes, until they are lightly browned and a toothpick inserted in centre comes out clean. Yields 18 large or 24 medium muffins.

BLUEBERRY BUTTERMILK MUFFINS

An excellent choice for weekend breakfasts, prepared with low-fat buttermilk these muffins will bring raves if you serve them hot from the oven accompanied by a cup or two of freshly brewed coffee.

1 cup low-fat buttermilk

1 egg

1/4 cup vegetable oil

2 cups all-purpose flour

1/4 cup sugar

2 1/2 teaspoons baking powder

1/2 teaspoon baking soda

1 teaspoon salt

1 cup wild blueberries

Preheat oven to 400°F. Whisk together buttermilk, egg and oil. Mix flour, sugar, baking powder, baking soda and salt together in a large bowl; stir in buttermilk mixture until just blended. Carefully fold in blue-berries and pour into prepared muffin tins. Bake for 20–25 minutes. Yields 12 large muffins.

BLUEBERRY LEMON MUFFINS

If you want to keep some of these muffins for breakfast, you would be well advised to hide them. They are simply the best blueberry muffins we have ever tasted.

2 cups flour

1/2 cup sugar

1/2 teaspoon salt

1 tablespoon baking powder

1 egg, beaten

zest of one lemon (thinly grated rind)

1 cup milk

1/2 cup butter, melted

1 1/4 cup fresh or frozen blueberries

1/4 cup butter, melted (2nd amount)

1 tablespoon lemon juice

1/4 cup sugar (2nd amount)

Preheat oven to 400°F. Sift flour, sugar, salt and baking powder into a large bowl. Whisk beaten egg, lemon zest, milk and melted butter and stir into dry ingredients until just blended. Stir in blueberries. Fill prepared muffin tins 2/3 full and bake for 20 minutes.

While muffins are baking combine melted butter and lemon juice in a small bowl. Measure sugar in a separate bowl. When muffins are slightly cooled dip top; first in lemon butter and then in sugar. Yields 18 muffins.

BLUEBERRY WAFFLES

Crispy nut-brown waffles are a nice variation from pancakes at Sunday brunch. Treat yourself and cover them with butter and your favourite syrup.

1 1/2 cups flour

2 tablespoons sugar

1/2 teaspoon salt

1/2 teaspoon baking soda

1 teaspoon baking powder

1 1/2 cups buttermilk

2 eggs, beaten

1/4 cup vegetable oil or melted butter

1/2 cup blueberries, washed and dried

Combine flour, sugar, salt, baking soda and baking powder in a large bowl. In another bowl whisk together buttermilk, eggs and oil. Add liquid to dry ingredients stirring only until smooth.

Preheat waffle iron according to manufacturer's directions. Pour batter onto hot waffle iron and sprinkle with 1 tablespoon blueberries. Bake until steaming stops and waffle is golden. Serve immediately. Serves 4.

BLUEBERRY PANCAKES

We make these pancakes year-round using "individually quick frozen" berries, and suggest you serve them with a topping of pure Maritime maple syrup.

1 cup flour

2 1/2 teaspoons baking powder

1 tablespoon sugar, optional

1 teaspoon salt

1 egg

1 cup milk

1 tablespoon vegetable oil

1/2 cup fresh or quick frozen wild blueberries

Combine flour, baking powder, sugar and salt in a large bowl. In a separate bowl, whisk together egg, milk and oil. Pour into flour mixture and mix until just blended. Stir in blueberries and drop by the spoonful on a hot griddle. Yields 8–10 small pancakes.

BUTTERMILK BLUEBERRY PANCAKES

We have been making these pancakes for so long that the recipe is firmly imprinted in our memory. Once you try them they will become the pancake of choice for your family as well!

1 1/2 cups flour

1 teaspoon baking powder

1/2 teaspoon salt

1/2 teaspoon baking soda

2 tablespoons sugar

1 3/4 cups buttermilk

2 tablespoons vegetable oil

1 egg

1/2 cup blueberries, fresh or frozen

Sift flour, baking powder, salt, baking soda and sugar into a large bowl. In another bowl, beat together buttermilk, vegetable oil and egg. Add liquid to flour mixture stirring, only until combined. Drop by large spoonful onto a greased hot griddle and sprinkle with blueberries. Cook until pancake bubbles; turn and cook on other side until golden brown. Serve hot with syrup of choice.

Yields 10–12 medium pancakes.

STARTERS & ACCOMPANIMENTS

Blueberries are more than just dessert. Maritime chefs have found ways to make them a versatile ingredient. Be sure to try Iced Blueberry Soup or Donna Laceby's Blueberry Vinaigrette served on assorted greens.

◄ *Donna Laceby's Assorted Greens with Blueberry Vinaigrette at Amherst Shore Country Inn, Lorneville, NS, is unforgettable.*

ASSORTED GREENS WITH BLUEBERRY VINAIGRETTE

AMHERST SHORE COUNTRY INN, LORNEVILLE, NS

This salad has great eye-appeal because of its unique colours (see photo, page 12).
If fresh blueberries are not available for the salad the chef suggests using
chopped celery or halved green or red seedless grapes.

10 to 12 cups assorted greens: any combination of romaine, spinach, red, oak or regular green leaf lettuce.

2 firm apples

1 cup fresh blueberries

Blueberry Vinaigrette (recipe follows)

Wash and dry greens; tear into medium-size pieces. Core apples, but do not peel; slice in thin strips on top of lettuce. Sprinkle fresh blueberries on top. Drizzle with 2–3 tablespoons Blueberry Vinaigrette. Makes 6–8 servings.

Blueberry Vinaigrette

1/2 cup olive oil

1/4 cup cider vinegar

1/8 teaspoon minced fresh garlic

1/2 teaspoon finely chopped green pepper

1/2 teaspoon finely chopped onion

1 teaspoon granulated sugar

1 cup fresh or frozen blueberries

Place all vinaigrette ingredients in a food processor and blend until vegetables are pureed. Strain through a sieve to remove small seeds. Refrigerate dressing until needed. Makes about 1 1/2 cups.

ICED BLUEBERRY SOUP

Try this very attractive soup served ice cold on a warm summer's day.

5 cups blueberries, washed and dried

2/3 cup water

1/2 cup dry white wine

1/4 cup extra fine, caster sugar*

1/4 teaspoon allspice

grating of nutmeg

1/2 teaspoon fresh lemon juice

1 1/4 cups buttermilk

Prepare blueberries and set aside 1/4 cup for garnish. Purée berries, water and wine in a food processor. Strain puree through a fine mesh strainer into a large bowl.

Stir sugar, cinnamon, nutmeg, lemon juice and buttermilk into blueberry purée. Refrigerate 4–5 hours for soup to blend flavours. Serve chilled garnished with reserved fresh blueberries. Serves 4–6.

* If you cannot buy commercial caster (superfine) sugar, prepare your own by crushing regular granulated sugar in a food processor until very fine.

BLUEBERRY VINEGAR

Drizzle this unique blue vinegar over salads or use as a meat marinade. Make one bottle for yourself and two to give away to lucky friends.

1 1/2 cups fresh or frozen blueberries

2 cups cider vinegar

1 cup dry red wine

3 cinnamon sticks

3 8-ounce fancy bottles, sterilized

Rinse and drain fresh berries or thaw frozen. Reserve 3 tablespoons whole berries and combine remaining berries with vinegar and wine in a large bowl. Cover and let stand overnight.

Heat vinegar mixture to a boil in an enamelled or stainless steel saucepan. Boil, uncovered, for 4 minutes. Remove from heat and strain. Place 1 cinnamon stick and 1 tablespoon reserved berries in each sterilized bottle. Pour hot vinegar into bottles, cover tightly and store in a cool dark place for 3 weeks before using. Refrigerate after opening. Yields three 8-ounce bottles.

BLUEBERRY TEA

BELLHILL TEA HOUSE, CANNING, NS

Serve this delightfully different tea to special friends. The aroma is wonderful and oh, so soothing.

1 pot of prepared orange pekoe tea

Amaretto liqueur

Grand Marnier liqueur

fresh blueberries

Brew fresh tea and add 1/2 ounce Amaretto, 1/2 ounce Grand Marnier and a few fresh blueberries to each serving.

BLUEBERRY CHUTNEY

Chutneys are wonderful staples to have on hand at the back of your refrigerator. Use them to jazz up an ordinary meat or seafood dish or to make an impromptu appetizer. Simply pour a generous amount of this colourful blue chutney over a block of soft cheese and serve with assorted crackers.

1/2 cup brown sugar, firmly packed

1/4 teaspoon cinnamon

1/8 teaspoon red pepper flakes

4 whole cloves

1/8 teaspoon nutmeg, freshly grated

1/2 cup red wine vinegar

1/2 cup orange juice

1/4 cup crystallized ginger, finely chopped

1/2 cup dried apricots, chopped

1/2 cup raisins

2 lemons, juice and zest (thinly grated rind)

4 cups blueberries, fresh or frozen

Combine all ingredients in a large saucepan. Bring the chutney to a boil, stirring constantly, until sugar is dissolved. Cover, reduce heat and simmer, stirring occasionally, until fruit is tender and thickened. Seal in sterilized jars. Makes 3 8-ounce jars.

MAIN COURSES

Always anxious to use local ingredients, Maritime chefs have developed wonderful recipes incorporating blueberries. They have found that this flavourful berry enhances pork and poultry dishes.

◄ *Amherst Shore Chicken with Blueberry Sauce from the kitchen of Donna Laceby at Amherst Shore Country Inn.*

ROAST LOIN OF PORK WITH BLUEBERRY AND JUNIPER SAUCE

THE DUNES CAFÉ AND GARDENS, BRACKLEY BEACH, PEI

*Chef Scott Carr at The Dunes Café serves roast loin of pork napped with
a blueberry demi-glace sauce (see photo opposite). To aid the home cook,
we are offering instructions using a commercial demi-glace mix.*

3–4 pound pork loin, deboned and tied

1 package demi-glace (available in most grocery stores)

1 1/4 cups cold water

1/4 cup red wine vinegar

1/4 cup red wine

1/4 cup blueberries

8 juniper berries or 1 ounce gin

l large sprig fresh thyme

6 black peppercorns

1 small bay leaf

salt and pepper, to taste

1/2 cup fresh blueberries (2nd amount)

Remove pork loin from refrigerator and allow to come to room temperature. Bake in a preheated 325°F oven allowing 30 minutes per pound or until a meat thermometer registers 170°F when inserted into the thickest part of the roast. Remove from oven and tent with foil.

While roast is baking, stir contents of demi-glace package into cold water and bring to a boil over medium-high heat. Reduce heat and cook until thickened. Reserve. In a separate pot combine red wine vinegar, red wine, 1/4 cup blueberries, juniper berries, thyme, peppercorns and bay leaf. Boil until liquid is reduced by two-thirds. Strain into reserved demi-glace and stir in second amount of blueberries. Return to heat, bring to serving temperature and season with salt and pepper. Serve with slices of roasted pork loin.
Serves 6.

*Chef Scott Carr presents his Roast Loin Pork with Blueberry and Juniper Sauce at ▶
the Dunes Café and Gardens, Brackley Beach, PEI.*

ROAST DUCK MARSHLANDS

MARSHLANDS INN, SACKVILLE, NB

*This rendition of roast duck (see photo opposite) is an easily prepared elegant meal
with a distinctively Maritime flavour. The blueberries can be stewed in
advance and incorporated into the sauce at serving time.*

1 duck (4 1/2 to 5 pounds)

salt

2 small apples, halved

2 small onions, halved

2 cups fresh blueberries

2 tablespoons water

1/2 cup sugar

1/4 cup vinegar

1/2 cup red wine

salt and pepper to taste

Preheat oven to 450°F. Rinse and pat dry a large duck. Season with salt and stuff with apple and onion pieces. Tie legs together with butcher's twine so duck will keep its shape while baking. Prick all over to release fat during cooking, and place on a rack in a roasting pan. Place duck in oven and immediately reduce temperature to 350°F. Cook until tender and juices from the thickest part of the thigh run clear, about 20 minutes per pound. Remove to a platter and tent with foil.

While duck is roasting stew blueberries with water and sugar. Set aside. Drain fat from roasting pan, being careful to conserve the brown drippings. Put pan over high heat and deglaze with vinegar; add wine and continue scraping brown bits from pan. Reduce by half and add stewed blueberries; season with salt and pepper and simmer 5 minutes longer to further reduce sauce. Serve carved duck napped with sauce. Serves 2–3.

*A tempting entrée of roast duck featuring Maritime blueberry sauce ▶
from Marshlands Inn, Sackville, NB.*

AMHERST SHORE CHICKEN WITH BLUEBERRY SAUCE

AMHERST SHORE COUNTRY INN, LORNEVILLE, NS

Cumberland County blueberries are at their peak during August and Donna Laceby uses them innovatively in several recipes. We are sure this will be one of your favourites.

4 boneless chicken breasts, 5-ounce portions

2 tablespoons cornstarch

3 tablespoons water

2 cups fresh or frozen blueberries

3 tablespoons sugar

1/2 cup dry red wine

zest of 1 lemon (thinly grated rind)

Preheat oven to 375°F. Rinse and pat dry chicken breasts. Over medium-high heat grill breasts until browned, turning once. Remove to oven and bake for 5–7 minutes, or until chicken is no longer pink in the centre.

Dissolve cornstarch in water and combine with blueberries and sugar in a saucepan. Cook over medium-high heat until berries break down and sauce thickens. Add wine and bring back to a boil. To serve, spread a small amount of blueberry sauce on each plate, top with chicken breast and drizzle with remaining sauce. Sprinkle with lemon zest to garnish. Serves 4.

Amherst Shore Chicken with Blueberry Sauce, one of Donna Laceby's tasty creations ▼

MEDALLIONS OF PORK WITH A CREAMY BLUEBERRY SAUCE

Ask your butcher to cut fairly large tenderloins, about 12–14 ounces each. This will provide the right sized medallions to ensure an elegant presentation.

2 pork tenderloins, 12–14 ounces each

1 1/2 tablespoons butter

1/2 small onion, diced

1/4 cup brandy

1 cup beef broth

1/2 teaspoon parsley

1/2 cup heavy cream (35% mf)

1/3 cup fresh blueberries

2 teaspoons butter

1 tablespoon flour

Trim tenderloins of any fat and slice into 1-inch medallions. Melt butter in a heavy skillet and sauté medallions until golden brown, turning once. Remove to an ovenproof platter and keep warm in a 225°F oven.

In the same pan, sauté onion until tender. Deglaze skillet with brandy, being careful to scrape up all brown bits. Stir in beef broth and parsley and bring to a boil. Boil briskly until mixture is reduced by one-third. Stir in cream and blueberries, bring to a boil and simmer 2 or 3 minutes. Knead together the butter and flour. Form into small balls and add to boiling sauce, one at a time, stirring constantly, until sauce reaches the consistency of heavy cream. Divide tenderloins between plates and nap with sauce. Serves 4.

DESSERTS

*A*h, what you have been waiting for! The endless array of decadent blueberry desserts. Need we say any more? For a light conclusion, try the Keltic Lodge Blueberry Sorbet. But to really impress your dinner guests, serve Blueberry Ballerina in the style of the Inn on the Cove, Saint John.

◄ *Cumberland County blueberries are at their best served in a Blueberry Flan from Amherst Shore Country Inn, Lorneville, NS.*

BLUEBERRY SPICE CHIFFON CAKE

GOWRIE HOUSE COUNTRY INN, SYDNEY MINES, NS

Clifford Matthews of Gowrie House tells us that this cake is equally delicious when made with fresh strawberries and decadent when made with fresh raspberries. We can't wait to try his suggestions!

2 1/4 cups cake flour

1 1/2 cups sugar

1 tablespoon baking powder

1 teaspoon cinnamon

3/4 teaspoon salt

6 eggs, separated

1/2 cup vegetable oil

3/4 cup water

1 1/2 teaspoon vanilla

1/4 teaspoon cream of tartar

1 cup heavy cream (35% mf)

2 tablespoons brown sugar

1 quart fresh blueberries

2 cups heavy cream (35% mf) (2nd amount)

1/4 cup sugar

Preheat oven to 325°F. Combine flour, 1 cup of the sugar, baking powder, cinnamon and salt in a large mixing bowl. Separate eggs. Combine yolks, oil, water and vanilla in a small bowl. In a large metal bowl beat egg whites with cream of tartar at medium speed until soft peaks form. Gradually beat in remaining half cup of sugar, a tablespoon at a time, beating at high speed until stiff peaks form.

Combine egg yolk mixture with flour mixture beating just until smooth. Carefully fold egg whites into cake batter, in four additions. Pour into an ungreased 10-inch tube pan and bake 1 hour and 10 minutes. Remove from oven and cool on a wire rack. When completely cooled, loosen around edges and invert on rack.

To assemble, slice cake in half. Using the lower half of the cake, cut a 2-inch tunnel in centre of cake about 1/2 inch from the sides. Remove excess cake with a fork to form a tunnel. Whip 1 cup of heavy cream with brown sugar until stiff peaks form. Fold in blueberries, reserving 1/4 cup for garnish. Fill tunnel and gently cover with upper half of cake. Whip remaining 2 cups of heavy cream with 1/4 cup of sugar and decorate cake. Garnish with reserved berries. Serves 12.

BLOMIDON INN BLUEBERRY SHORTCAKE

BLOMIDON INN, WOLFVILLE, NS

"This is no ordinary shortcake," states Jim Laceby, owner of Blomidon Inn. Diners agree with the claim, making it one of the more popular desserts during berry season.

Shortcakes

1/4 cup softened butter

3 tablespoons sugar

2 eggs

1 tablespoon lemon zest (thinly grated rind)

2 tablespoons fresh lemon juice

1/2 cup blend (10% mf)

2 cups flour

1 tablespoon baking powder

pinch of salt

Preheat oven to 375°F. Cream butter and sugar together in the bowl of a mixer, until light and fluffy. Beat in eggs, lemon zest and lemon juice and blend. Sift flour, baking powder and salt together and gradually mix into the egg mixture being careful not to overmix. Turn shortcake out onto a floured surface, turn to coat other side and gently press to 3/4-inch thickness. Cut shortcakes with a 3-inch cutter, and place on an ungreased cookie sheet 1 1/2 inches apart. Bake for 15 minutes or until puffed and lightly browned on the bottom. Cool on wire racks.

To serve, split shortcake, spoon Blomidon Inn Blueberry Sauce onto the bottom half and place the top of the shortcake on top as a cover. Garnish with Crème Anglaise and sifted icing sugar. Serves 6–8.

Blomidon Inn Blueberry Sauce

2 cups fresh blueberries

3/4 cup sugar

1/2 cup water

1 tablespoon cornstarch

Combine blueberries, sugar and a little of the water in a heavy saucepan over medium heat; cook and stir until the berries collapse. Continue to heat until a boil is reached. Combine cornstarch and remaining water and whisk into the sauce. Return to boiling and cook until sauce is thickened. Remove from heat and cool.

Crème Anglaise *(supplied by authors)*

1/2 cup heavy cream (35% mf)

1/2 cup milk

yolks of 2 eggs

4 tablespoons icing sugar

Heat, but do not boil, the cream and milk in the top of a double boiler over hot water. (If preferred, use 1 cup of milk and omit the 1/2 cup of heavy cream). Whisk together yolks and icing sugar. Stir a small amount of the hot mixture into the yolks, return yolks to hot mixture and cook gently until mixture lightly coats the back of a spoon. Remove from heat, cover with plastic wrap and chill. Yields 1 cup.

BLUEBERRY FLAN

AMHERST SHORE COUNTRY INN, LORNEVILLE, NS

Donna Laceby at the Amherst Shore Country Inn suggests adding a little tapioca to absorb some of the juices if you are using frozen blueberries. For a lighter dessert use low-fat sour cream and omit the whipped cream garnish.

Crust

1 1/2 cups flour

1/2 cup sugar

1 1/2 teaspoons baking powder

1/2 cup butter, softened

1 egg

1/2 teaspoon almond extract

Filling

5 cups fresh or frozen (unthawed) blueberries

2 tablespoons orange liqueur

1 teaspoon lemon zest (thinly grated rind)

4 teaspoons minute tapioca, if using frozen berries

Topping

2 cups sour cream

1/2 cup sugar

2 egg yolks

1/2 teaspoon almond extract

2/3 cup heavy cream (35% mf), whipped for garnish

Preheat oven to 350°F. To prepare crust, blend flour, sugar, baking powder and butter in a mixing bowl. Add egg and almond extract and blend. Pat dough over the base of a greased 10 1/2-inch springform pan.

Mix together blueberries, liqueur, lemon zest and minute tapioca, if using frozen berries. Spoon onto crust.

Combine topping ingredients and mix well. Spoon evenly over blueberries in crust. Bake at 350°F for 1 1/4 hours or until crust is golden and berries are tender. Let cool, then refrigerate. Just before serving, top generously with whipped cream. Serves 10–12.

Blueberry Flan from Amherst Shore Country Inn, Lorneville, NS. ▶

BLUEBERRY BALLERINA

INN ON THE COVE, SAINT JOHN, NB

This spectacular dessert (see photo opposite) is easy to prepare and is a variation of the famous Pavlova which uses strawberries and kiwi fruit. The meringue is best made when the humidity is low.

Meringue

4–6 egg whites, at room temperature

pinch of cream of tartar

1 cup white sugar

1 tablespoon cornstarch

pinch of salt

1 teaspoon vanilla

2 teaspoons cider vinegar

1 cup heavy cream (35% mf), whipped with 1 tablespoon sugar

1 1/2 cup fresh blueberries

Blueberry Coulis (recipe follows)

Preheat oven to 400°F. Beat egg whites and cream of tartar while gradually adding sugar. When all sugar is incorporated continue to beat until whites are very stiff. Fold in cornstarch and salt. Mix in vanilla and vinegar.

Cut two pieces of waxed paper to fit a large baking sheet. Thoroughly wet waxed paper sheets with cold water and place on baking sheet. Pile meringue in a circle with the sides slightly higher than the centre. Place in preheated 400°F oven and immediately turn off heat. Leave in oven 1 1/2 hours. Remove, let stand 10 minutes then separate from waxed paper and cool.

Place meringue on serving plate, fill with sweetened whipped cream and top with blueberries. Serve individual portions drizzled with Blueberry Coulis. Serves 8–10.

Blueberry Coulis *(supplied by authors)*

2 cups fresh or frozen blueberries

1/2 cup white sugar, or to taste

1/4 cup water

2 teaspoons cornstarch, dissolved in 1 tablespoon cold water

2 teaspoons fresh lemon juice

In a heavy saucepan bring blueberries, sugar and water to a boil, stirring occasionally, 5 minutes. Prepare cornstarch mixture and stir into pan. Add lemon juice and simmer, 2 minutes, stirring constantly. Strain sauce, then chill until cold. To serve, mound meringue with whipped cream, sprinkle with fresh berries and drizzle with blueberry sauce.

The one and only Blueberry Ballerina created by Willa and Ross Mavis ▶ at the Inn on the Cove, Saint John, NB.

WARM FRUIT COMPOTE

THE PINES RESORT HOTEL, DIGBY, NS

Chefs at the Pines serve this delightful blend of fresh fruits in a baked phyllo shell or as a filling for dessert crèpes. We also tried it spooned over frozen yoghurt or vanilla ice cream!

3/4 cup fresh cranberries

3/4 cup pears, peeled and diced

3/4 cup apples, peeled and diced

1/4 cup fresh blueberries

1/4 cup brown sugar

1/8 teaspoon cloves

1/8 teaspoon allspice

1/4 teaspoon cinnamon

whipped cream as garnish

Combine all ingredients in a large saucepan and cook slowly 5–7 minutes, stirring occasionally. Serve in a phyllo shell with a dollop of whipped cream or as a basis for other desserts. Serves 4–6.

You will be delighted with Warm Fruit Compote served in a phyllo cup ▶
at the Pines Resort Hotel, Digby, NS.

BLUEBERRY GRUNT

MOUNTAIN GAP INN AND RESORT, SMITH'S COVE, NS

*Blueberry Grunt is the homey kind of dessert that stretches
almost as far as Maritime hospitality.*

Sauce

2 cups fresh or frozen blueberries

1/4 – 1/2 cup sugar

1/3 cup water

Dumplings

1 cup flour

2 teaspoons baking powder

1 teaspoon sugar

1/4 teaspoon salt

1/2 tablespoon butter

1/2 tablespoon shortening

1/3 – 1/2 cup milk

vanilla ice cream or whipped cream for
garnish

Wash and drain berries, combine with sugar and water and bring to a boil in a large saucepan. Reduce heat and simmer until berries are soft and sauce begins to thicken, about 5 minutes.

Whisk together flour, baking powder, sugar and salt. Cut in butter and shortening with a pastry blender. Stir in just enough milk to make a soft dough. Drop the batter by tablespoons on top of the simmering berry sauce. Immediately cover saucepan and cook over medium heat without removing cover for 15–18 minutes. At Mountain Gap, this delicious dessert is served warm with vanilla ice cream or a dollop of whipped cream. Serves 4–6.

*Summer just wouldn't be the same without it — Maritime Blueberry Grunt ▶
served at Mountain Gap Inn and Resort, Smith's Cove, NS.*

CARAMEL CHOCOLATE CRÈME WITH WARM BLUEBERRY SAUCE

DUFFERIN INN AND SAN MARTELLO DININGROOM, SAINT JOHN, NB

Margret and Axel Begner serve this decadent crème caramel topped with a warm blueberry sauce. The subtle addition of chocolate to the custard makes it a memorable dessert!

1/2 cup sugar

1 tablespoon water

1 cup milk

1 cup heavy cream (35% mf)

2 squares white chocolate

3 egg yolks

2 whole eggs

Blueberry Sauce (recipe follows)

Note: Caramel reaches a very high temperature. We suggest you use oven mitts to protect yourself from splattering when the milk and cream are added.

Heat sugar and water in a heavy saucepan over low heat, shaking the pan occasionally until the sugar is dissolved. Turn heat to high and boil, without stirring, until caramel is golden brown. Watch carefully so that it does not burn. Remove from heat and cautiously stir in the milk and cream. Return to heat and bring, almost to a boil; add chocolate and stir until melted.

Preheat oven to 350°F. In a bowl combine yolks and whole eggs. Stir a small amount of the hot mixture into the eggs, return eggs to hot mixture and whisk to combine. Pour into six custard cups. Place custard cups in a water bath and bake in a preheated 350°F oven 30–35 minutes or until a knife inserted in the centre comes out clean. Cool, then chill. To serve, unmold on individual serving plates and top with warm blueberry sauce. Serves 6.

Blueberry Sauce

1 1/2 cup blueberries

1 cup red wine

4 tablespoons sugar

1 tablespoon cornstarch

1 teaspoon vanilla

Cook blueberries, wine, sugar and cornstarch in a saucepan over medium heat until thick and bubbly. Remove from heat, stir in vanilla and keep warm.

Caramel Chocolate Crème with Warm Blueberry Sauce is too good to be true, ▶
from the dining room of the Dufferin Inn, Saint John, NB.

BLUEBERRY APPLE FLAN

HADDON HALL, CHESTER, NS

The chef at Haddon Hall suggests that you may, for convenience, prepare the filling a day in advance. He also advises baking the flan on a cookie sheet, to avoid having the fruit bubble over into your oven.

Butter Pastry (Pâte Brise)

1 1/4 cups flour

1/4 teaspoon salt

1/2 cup unsalted butter, softened

3 tablespoons ice water

Combine flour and salt in a medium-sized bowl. Cut in butter with a pastry blender until the mixture resembles coarse meal. Sprinkle with enough water to hold dough together. Form into a ball, wrap in plastic wrap and refrigerate 30 minutes. Before removing from refrigerator, preheat oven to 400°F. Flatten dough between two sheets of plastic wrap to form a disc. Roll to fit a 10-inch flan pan. Prick pastry and bake for 15 minutes. Cool.

Filling

1 1/4 cup apple cider

1 scant cup sugar

1 1/4 cups fresh blueberries

4 medium cooking apples, peeled and sliced

Heat cider and sugar until sugar dissolves, then boil 2 minutes. Add blueberries and sliced apples and return to a boil. Reduce heat and simmer until apples are tender, about 5 minutes. Transfer to a bowl, chill and reserve.

Remove fruit from bowl with a slotted spoon and arrange over flan pastry. Top with streusel mixture (below) and bake at 400°F for 30–35 minutes, until topping has browned and filling is bubbling. Serves 6–8.

Streusel Topping

1/2 cup flour

1/3 cup dark brown sugar

1/3 cup unsalted butter

1/2 cup pecans, coarsely chopped

Combine flour, brown sugar and butter. Add pecan pieces and sprinkle over prepared flan.

Blueberry Apple Flan from Haddon Hall, Chester, NS. ▶

COLD BLUEBERRY SOUFFLÉ

LA PERLA RESTAURANT, DARTMOUTH, NS

This is an impressive dessert that is easy to prepare in advance. At La Perla it is presented in individual dishes decorated with a dollop of whipped cream, fresh mint leaves or spring flowers.

5 cups blueberries, fresh or frozen

2 tablespoons water

2 tablespoons Grand Marnier liqueur

1 1/2 package gelatin

3 egg whites

1/2 cup sugar

1 1/2 cup heavy cream (35% mf), whipped

Prepare a 3-cup soufflé dish with a foil collar.

In a deep saucepan cook blueberries and water over medium heat until berries have broken down and mixture has become a sauce. Remove from heat and stir in Grand Marnier. Keep warm.

In a small bowl sprinkle gelatin over 3 tablespoons of cold water and stir. Set aside 5 minutes to dissolve, then stir into blueberry sauce.

Bring a large pot of water to a rolling boil. Place a large steel bowl over the water, add egg whites and sugar; whisk until thick and sugar is completely dissolved. Remove from heat and place bowl over a large bowl of ice cubes. Carefully fold blueberry mixture into egg whites. Fold in whipped cream and pour into a prepared 3-quart soufflé dish. Refrigerate 4 hours, or until set. To serve, remove foil collar and decorate as desired.

A decadent serving Cold Blueberry Soufflé from LaPerla Restaurant, Dartmouth, NS. ▶

BLUEBERRY ORANGE COMPOTE WITH LEMONADE SAUCE AND CINNAMON ICE CREAM IN A CRISP COOKIE CUP

INN AT BAY FORTUNE, BAY FORTUNE, PEI

Chef Michael Smith has created a winner and a work of art (see photo opposite). The flavours and textures of this delightful dessert are simply "sinful."

Compote

2 oranges

2 cups blueberries

2 tablespoons Grand Marnier liqueur

1/4 cup icing sugar, sifted

Zest (thinly grated peel), peel and section oranges being careful to discard all pith. Combine zest, orange sections, blueberries, Grand Marnier and icing sugar in a bowl. Cover and reserve for 1/2 hour to allow flavours to blend.

Lemonade Sauce

1/3 cup sugar

2 lemons, zest (thinly grated peel) and juice

1/3 cup water

2 medium apples, cored and chopped

Combine sugar, lemon zest, juice, water and apples in a small saucepan. Bring to a boil, stirring until sugar dissolves; reduce heat and simmer for 15 minutes. Purée in a blender until sauce is smooth and then strain through a fine mesh strainer. Reserve and cool.

Crisp Cookie Cups

1/4 cup butter

1/4 cup corn syrup

2 1/2 tablespoons brown sugar

1/3 cup cake flour

1/2 cup ground walnuts

Preheat oven to 350°F. In a heavy saucepan, combine butter, corn syrup and sugar over medium heat; bring to a boil stirring constantly. Remove from heat. Combine flour and ground nuts and add to sugar mixture stirring to form a batter.

Drop tablespoons of batter onto greased baking sheets about 4 inches apart. Bake for 6–8 minutes, until golden brown and bubbly. Remove from oven and let cool for 30 seconds or until edges easily lift with a spatula. Immediately drape hot cookie over inverted custard cups, gently pressing to the form. (If cookies become too brittle to shape, return to oven just until softened.) Cool on wire racks. May be made up to 48 hours in advance and stored in an airtight container.

Cinnamon Ice Cream

1 pint good quality vanilla ice cream

1 tablespoon cinnamon-sugar

Stir cinnamon sugar into slightly softened ice cream. Return to freezer.

To serve: place Crisp Cookie Cup on serving plate. Fill with a scoop of Cinnamon Ice Cream, spoon Compote around ice cream and drizzle with Lemonade Sauce. Serves 6–8.

Blueberry Orange Compote, Inn at Bay Fortune, Bay Fortune, PEI. ▶

BLUEBERRY AND RHUBARB CRUMBLE

DALVAY-BY-THE-SEA, DALVAY, PEI

*Executive chef Richard Kemp of Dalvay-by-the-Sea serves this delicious
fruit dessert hot, with berry and yoghurt ice cream.*

Filling

2 tablespoons butter

2/3 cup sugar, or to taste

1 1/2 tablespoons lemon juice

1 pound rhubarb, chopped (3–4 cups)

1 cup blueberries

1/2 teaspoon cinnamon

1/2 teaspoon vanilla

Crumble

1/3 cup butter, softened

1/2 cup sugar

1/2 cup flour

1/2 cup ground almonds

1/3 cup rolled oats

In a saucepan combine butter, sugar and lemon juice; cook and stir over medium heat until lightly golden. Add rhubarb and increase heat to medium high. Cook and stir until it starts to thicken, approximately 10 minutes. Add blueberries and cinnamon and cook for an additional 4 minutes. Remove from heat, stir in vanilla and cool.

Preheat oven to 425°F. Cream butter and sugar until smooth. Combine flour, almonds and oats and gradually rub into butter mixture until crumbly. Pour rhubarb blueberry mixture into a greased two-quart baking dish and sprinkle crumble mixture on top. Bake for 25–30 minutes, until top is browned. (May also be baked in 6 individual ramekins at 425°F for 10–12 minutes.) Serve warm with ice cream or whipped cream. Serves 6.

Summer's bounty at its best, Blueberry and Rhubarb Crumble served at Dalvay-by-the-Sea, PEI. ▶

BLUEBERRY MAPLE CRISP

DRURY LANE STEAK HOUSE, AULAC, NB

Truly a Maritime recipe, this crisp is best served warm with vanilla ice cream and comes with a guarantee to satisfy the sweetest sweet tooth!

4 cups fresh blueberries

1/2 cup maple syrup

1 teaspoon cinnamon

1/4 cup cornstarch

1 1/4 cups flour

3/4 cup brown sugar

1/2 cup butter, softened

1 teaspoon almond extract

Preheat oven to 375°F. Combine blueberries, maple syrup, cinnamon and cornstarch and put in a lightly greased 9-inch square baking dish. In a bowl blend flour and sugar and cut in butter and almond extract to form a crumbly mixture. Sprinkle flour mixture over berries and bake for 30 minutes until lightly browned and bubbly around the edges. Serves 6–8.

Chef Sharon Meldrum's Blueberry Maple Crisp is a new twist on ▶ an old favourite, at Drury Lane Steak House, Aulac, NB.

50

CUMBERLAND BLUEBERRY SAUCE

This delicious sauce is simple to make and is very versatile. Serve it warm or cold over ice-cream, fresh fruits, angel food or pound cake. Yummy!

1/4 cup granulated sugar

3/4 teaspoon cinnamon

1/4 teaspoon nutmeg

1 1/2 cups fresh or frozen blueberries

Combine all ingredients in a saucepan and cook over low heat, stirring frequently until sauce boils and begins to thicken, approximately 10 minutes. Makes 2 cups.

WILD BLUEBERRY POSSET

ACTON'S GRILL AND CAFÉ, WOLFVILLE, NS

The chef at Acton's serves this refreshing dessert in a glass dish garnished with a few sprigs of fresh mint, whole fresh blueberries and some cookies on the side.

2 cups fresh wild blueberries, crushed

1/2 cup sugar

2 cups heavy cream (35% mf), whipped

2 tablespoons lemon juice

4 egg whites

Combine crushed blueberries with sugar, whipped cream and lemon juice. Set aside. Beat egg whites until stiff but not dry; carefully fold into blueberry and cream mixture. Spoon into individual dessert dishes and serve immediately. Yields 8 servings.

*Refreshing Wild Blueberry Posset served with tea cookies ▶
at Acton's Grill and Café, Wolfville, NS.*

Easy Blueberry Crème Brulée

QUACO INN, ST. MARTINS, NB

Innkeeper Betty Ann Murray provided this quick and easy dessert recipe that is oh, so tasty!

1 pint fresh blueberries

2/3 cup low-fat sour cream

1/2 cup plain yoghurt

1/3 cup brown sugar

Divide blueberries between 6 heat proof ramekins. Combine sour cream and yoghurt and spread over blueberries being careful to cover completely. Sprinkle brown sugar over sour cream and broil 3 inches from element until sugar caramelizes, approximately 3–5 minutes. Watch carefully as topping can easily burn. Serve immediately. Serves 6.

Fresh blueberries accompany Quaco Inn's Blueberry Crème Brulée, St. Martins, NB. ▼

FRESH BLUEBERRIES WITH MAPLE BRANDY CREAM

THE COMPASS ROSE INN, LUNENBURG, NS

This delightful recipe is low in fat, has an excellent refrigerator life and is very easy to prepare. The owners of Lunenburg's Compass Rose Inn like to serve it over all fresh seasonal fruits.

1 cup low-fat sour cream

1/4 cup maple syrup

2 tablespoons brandy

3 cups blueberries, washed and drained

In a bowl whisk together sour cream, maple syrup and brandy. Refrigerate. Serve drizzled over fresh blueberries. Makes 1 1/4 cups cream sauce. Serves 6.

BLUEBERRY SORBET

KELTIC LODGE, INGONISH, NS

The chefs at Keltic Lodge prepare their sorbets and ice creams using fresh seasonal fruit. This Blueberry Sorbet is simple to make and the flavour is delicate and refreshing.

2 cups water

4 teaspoons corn syrup

1 cup sugar

4 cups blueberries

2 tablespoons fresh lemon juice

In a saucepan bring water, corn syrup and sugar to boil over high heat, stirring constantly to dissolve the sugar. Boil for 1 minute, remove from heat and cool.

Purée berries in food processor until smooth. Combine prepared syrup, lemon juice and berries. Pour mixture into large shallow container and freeze until firm, approximately 4 hours. Return sorbet to food processor and process until smooth and creamy. Immediately pack sorbet into an airtight container and refreeze until firm. Makes 6 cups.

CLASSIC ENGLISH TRIFLE

THE GARRISON HOUSE INN, ANNAPOLIS ROYAL, NS

Patrick Redgrave of the Garrison House Inn prepares his trifle using many seasonal fruits.
We find that blueberries and bananas are a winning combination.

8–10 ladyfingers or 1 sponge cake

1/2 cup blueberry jam

1/4 cup sherry

1 1/2 cups sliced bananas

1 1/2 cups fresh blueberries

custard (recipe follows)

1/2 cup heavy cream

1/2 teaspoon vanilla

1/4 cup almonds, sliced

Split ladyfingers or cake and spread with thick layer of jam. Arrange pieces over the bottom of a shallow, clear glass bowl. Sprinkle with sherry. Arrange fruit on cake. Prepare custard and while still warm pour over trifle. Let stand at room temperature until cool, then refrigerate. To serve, whip cream until stiff and add vanilla. Spread over custard and top with almonds. Serves 6–8.

Custard *(supplied by authors)*

1/4 cup sugar

3 tablespoons flour

3 egg yolks, beaten

2 cups milk

2 teaspoons lemon zest (thinly grated peel)

1 teaspoon vanilla

In a heavy saucepan combine sugar, flour, egg yolks, milk and lemon zest. Cook, stirring over medium heat until mixture is thick and begins to boil. Remove from heat, add vanilla and cover with waxed paper.

CHEESECAKE TART WITH BLUEBERRY TOPPING

This is a variation of a recipe from the Bright House in Sherbrooke, NS
It is delicious served with any seasonal fruit sauce.

1 unbaked 10-inch pie shell

2/3 cup ricotta cheese

1/2 cup sour cream

1/2 cup milk

1 tablespoon lemon juice

grated zest of 1/2 lemon

1/4 teaspoon mace

1/2 teaspoon vanilla

2 tablespoons cornstarch

1 tablespoon butter, melted

2 eggs, separated

1/4 cup sugar

4 tablespoons sugar (2nd amount)

pinch of salt

Preheat oven to 400°F. Line a deep, 10-inch pie plate with pastry of your choice. Blend together cheese, sour cream, milk, lemon juice, zest, mace, vanilla, cornstarch, butter, egg yolks and sugar. Beat egg whites until stiff, adding second amount of sugar and salt. Fold egg whites into cheese mixture and pour into pie shell. Bake for 10 minutes, reduce temperature to 350°F and bake an additional 25 minutes or until set. Cool, then refrigerate and serve with blueberry topping. Serves 6–8.

Blueberry Topping

1 1/2 cup fresh blueberries

1/2 cup sugar

1/3 cup cold water

2 tablespoons cornstarch

1 tablespoon lemon juice

Combine blueberries, sugar, cornstarch and lemon juice in a heavy bottomed saucepan and place over medium heat. Stir constantly until sugar is dissolved. Bring to a boil and cook 3–5 minutes. Store in refrigerator until ready to serve.

BLUEBERRY GLACÉ TART

DUNCREIGAN COUNTRY INN, MABOU, NS

Eleanor Mullendore of the Duncreigan Country Inn tells us that as a variation, this recipe can be prepared with fresh strawberries or raspberries in season.

Tart Pastry

1 cup all purpose flour

1/3 cup pastry flour

1 tablespoon sugar

1/3 cup unsalted butter, chilled

2 tablespoons vegetable shortening, chilled

3 1/2 – 4 tablespoons ice water

Mix dry ingredients together in a bowl. Cut in butter and shortening with a pastry blender until mixture resembles coarse crumbs. Stir in cold water just until dough sticks together. Form into a smooth ball and wrap in plastic wrap; chill 30 minutes. Preheat oven to 425°F. Roll pastry to fit a 9-inch tart or pie plate and chill 15 minutes. Prick well and bake until golden, about 12–15 minutes. Remove from oven and cool.

Filling

3 cups fresh blueberries

3/4 cup sugar

1 tablespoon lime juice

1/2 cup cream cheese, softened

sweetened whipped cream as garnish (optional)

Cook 1 cup of the blueberries with the sugar until thickened. Purée until smooth, add lime juice and cool. Stir 1 1/2 cup of the remaining berries into sauce.

Spread cream cheese over cooled pastry shell. Top with berry mixture. Sprinkle remaining 1/2 cup berries over top and chill until set. Garnish with sweetened whipped cream. Serves 6–8.

◄ *Blueberry Glacé Tart from the dining room at Duncreigan Country Inn, Mabou, NS.* ►

BLUEBERRY GRAND MARNIER FLAN

THE FALCOURT INN, NICTAUX, NS

*Chef Robin Parker developed this recipe for the Falcourt Inn to utilize the
bountiful valley harvest of fresh blueberries.*

Pastry

1 cup + 1 tablespoon flour

1/4 cup sugar

dash of salt

3/4 teaspoon lemon zest (thinly grated peel)

1/4 cup butter, softened

2 egg yolks, beaten

Preheat oven to 350°F. Blend together the flour, sugar, salt and zest. Cut in butter and bind together with egg yolks. Press into the bottom and up the sides of a greased 10-inch flan pan. Bake for 10 minutes. Cool.

Filling

3/4 cup sugar

1/4 cup cornstarch

1 1/2 cups milk

2 eggs

1 tablespoon butter

1 teaspoon vanilla

1 1/2 tablespoons Grand Marnier liqueur

3 cups fresh blueberries

1/2 cup sugar (2nd amount)

3 tablespoons apricot jam melted with 1 teaspoon water

Preheat oven to 350°F. In the top half of a double boiler over simmering water combine sugar and cornstarch. Whisk in milk and bring to a boil, stirring constantly. In a small bowl beat eggs, stir in a little of the hot milk mixture then return to the double boiler and cook until thick and smooth. Remove from heat and stir in butter, vanilla and Grand Marnier. Pour into prepared flan pastry.

Mix together blueberries and sugar and sprinkle evenly over custard. Bake for 30–35 minutes, or until berries are cooked. Melt apricot jelly with water and brush over berries. Serve chilled with whipped cream for a garnish, if desired. Serves 6–8.

INGONISH BLUEBERRY CLAFOUTI

KELTIC LODGE, INGONISH, NS

The chefs at Keltic Lodge use fresh local blueberries in this variation of a traditional cherry clafouti. Serve it warm, plain or with a dollop of fresh whipped cream.

1 single pie crust (recipe follows)

1/2 cup milk

1/2 cup plain yoghurt

3/4 cup sugar

4 eggs, beaten

1 1/2 teaspoon vanilla

3 cups fresh blueberries

Preheat oven to 375°F. Prepare pastry and arrange in a 9-inch diameter, 3/4-inch deep, loose bottomed flan or pie pan. Prick the crust with a fork and bake for 12 minutes.

In a saucepan, bring milk, yoghurt and sugar to a boil stirring constantly. Stir small amount of hot mixture into eggs, return to hot mixture and cook until thickened, stirring constantly. Remove from heat and stir in vanilla. Add blueberries to prepared pastry shell and pour custard over. Bake for 25 minutes. Serve warm.

Single Shell Pastry

1 cup flour

1/4 teaspoon salt

1/2 cup shortening

2–3 tablespoons cold water

Combine flour and salt in mixing bowl. Cut shortening into flour with pastry blender until mixture is size of large peas. Do not overmix. Sprinkle cold water over mixture and blend with a fork until absorbed. Form into a ball and roll out on a floured surface. Yields enough pastry for single shell.